When they say 'they sure do grow up fast,'
take their word for it. It's true.

Each page of this book was delicately crafted, illustrated, and painted by hand by a single artist located in Kingwood, TX. Learn more about the artist in the back of this book.

HOW TO USE THIS BOOK

To get the most out of using Growing Up, *please read the following instructions.*

From kindergarten through high school, there is ample room in this book for you to document your child's educational journey. Each section gives you space to document your child's hopes, wishes, likes, dislikes, and more during that time in their life. On the opening page for each section, there is a blank line at the bottom for you to record the dates of that particular school year (for example: 2023-2024). On the following page, you'll find a list of questions that you can ask your child on the first day of school, or at the start of the year. You'll also find a page for you to add your child's official school photo (as precious or as awkward as it may be!), as well as room to include a favorite project or piece of artwork they completed during the year. Your child's birthday also has its own special page, where you can document how it was celebrated that year as well. There is also additional room at the end of each section that you can use to save additional photos (such as the first day of school photo), artwork, notes, etc. from that year. Lastly, the final page of each section is a dedicated journaling page, where a parent or guardian can write a letter to your child—sharing thoughts, changes, experiences, or advice as you watch them grow up.

There is a pocket in the back to hold additional cherished mementos from childhood: notes from teachers, photographs, artwork, accomplishments, and so on.

For quality and consistency, I recommend that you use a black archival ink pen to write with. I prefer Micron pens.

I would love to see how you document your memories in your copy of Growing Up!
Tag #GrowingUpBOOK and @korieherold to connect on social media.

Korie Herold

Growing Up

A MODERN MEMORY BOOK FOR THE SCHOOL YEARS

Korie Herold

Paige Tate & Co.

Paige Tate & Co.

Published by Paige Tate & Co., an imprint of Blue Star Press
PO Box 8835, Bend, OR 97708
contact@paigetate.com | www.paigetate.com

The authorized representative in the EU for product safety and compliance is Authorised Rep Compliance Ltd., Ground Floor, 71 Lower Baggot Street, Dublin, D02 P593, Ireland. www.arccompliance.com.

Illustrations and Design by Korie Herold

ISBN: 9781944515966
Printed in China
10 9 8 7 6 5 4 3

K

kindergarten

Date:

1st Day of School

The Kindergarten Edition

What do you want to be when you grow up and why?

How tall are you?

Favorite color :

Favorite food :

Favorite toy or possession :

Favorite book :

Favorite movie/show :

Who are your teachers this year?

What do you enjoy learning about most?

What is your favorite thing to do after school?

Who are some of your friends?

Who do you spend the most time with?

What are three words you'd use to describe yourself?

What makes you happy?

What makes you feel the most loved?

What do you like to do to make others feel loved?

Are you scared or afraid of anything?

What is your favorite thing you did this summer?

If you could have one wish, what would it be?

What are you looking forward to most this year?

Add Photo Here!

Picture Day!

Picture day at school went like this :

Leave your Mark!

A project or piece of art you created this year :

Your signature :

Something memorable that happened :

New friends made this year :

Things you learned :

Extracurriculars :

Biggest accomplishment this year :

Highlight of the school year :

My Birthday!

Add Photo Here!

This is how we celebrated your birthday this year :

As you grow...

A note from:

first grade

1st Day of School

The First Grade Edition

Date:

What do you want to be when you grow up and why?

How tall are you?

Favorite color :

Favorite food :

Favorite toy or possession :

Favorite book :

Favorite movie/show :

Who are your teachers this year?

What do you enjoy learning about most?

What is your favorite thing to do after school?

Who are some of your friends?

Who do you spend the most time with?

What are three words you'd use to describe yourself?

What makes you happy?

What makes you feel the most loved?

What do you like to do to make others feel loved?

Are you scared or afraid of anything?

What is your favorite thing you did this summer?

If you could have one wish, what would it be?

What are you looking forward to most this year?

Picture Day!

Picture day at school went like this :

Leave your Mark!

A project or piece of art you created this year :

Your signature :

Something memorable that happened :

New friends made this year :

Things you learned :

Extracurriculars :

Biggest accomplishment this year :

Highlight of the school year :

My Birthday!

Add Photo Here!

This is how we celebrated your birthday this year :

As you grow...

A note from:

Second grade

1st Day of School

The Second Grade Edition

Date:

What do you want to be when you grow up and why?

How tall are you?

Favorite color :

Favorite food :

Favorite toy or possession :

Favorite book :

Favorite movie/show :

Who are your teachers this year?

What do you enjoy learning about most?

What is your favorite thing to do after school?

Who are some of your friends?

Who do you spend the most time with?

What are three words you'd use to describe yourself?

What makes you happy?

What makes you feel the most loved?

What do you like to do to make others feel loved?

Are you scared or afraid of anything?

What is your favorite thing you did this summer?

If you could have one wish, what would it be?

What are you looking forward to most this year?

Picture Day!

Picture day at school went like this :

Leave your Mark!

A project or piece of art you created this year :

Your signature :

Something memorable that happened :

New friends made this year :

Things you learned :

Extracurriculars :

Biggest accomplishment this year :

Highlight of the school year :

My Birthday!

Add Photo Here!

This is how we celebrated your birthday this year :

As you grow...

A note from:

third grade

1st Day of School

Date:

The Third Grade Edition

What do you want to be when you grow up and why?

How tall are you?

Favorite color :

Favorite food :

Favorite toy or possession :

Favorite book :

Favorite movie/show :

Who are your teachers this year?

What do you enjoy learning about most?

What is your favorite thing to do after school?

Who are some of your friends?

Who do you spend the most time with?

What are three words you'd use to describe yourself?

What makes you happy?

What makes you feel the most loved?

What do you like to do to make others feel loved?

Are you scared or afraid of anything?

What is your favorite thing you did this summer?

If you could have one wish, what would it be?

What are you looking forward to most this year?

Add Photo Here!

Picture Day!

Picture day at school went like this :

Leave your Mark!

A project or piece of art you created this year :

Your signature :

Something memorable that happened :

New friends made this year :

Things you learned :

Extracurriculars :

Biggest accomplishment this year :

Highlight of the school year :

My Birthday!

Add Photo Here!

This is how we celebrated your birthday this year :

As you grow...

A note from:

fourth grade

1st Day of School

Date:

The Fourth Grade Edition

What do you want to be when you grow up and why?

How tall are you?

Favorite color :

Favorite food :

Favorite toy or possession :

Favorite book :

Favorite movie/show :

Who are your teachers this year?

What do you enjoy learning about most?

What is your favorite thing to do after school?

Who are some of your friends?

Who do you spend the most time with?

What are three words you'd use to describe yourself?

What makes you happy?

What makes you feel the most loved?

What do you like to do to make others feel loved?

Are you scared or afraid of anything?

What is your favorite thing you did this summer?

If you could have one wish, what would it be?

What are you looking forward to most this year?

Picture Day!

Picture day at school went like this : ____________________

____

____

Leave your Mark!

A project or piece of art you created this year :

Your signature :

Something memorable that happened :

New friends made this year :

Things you learned :

Extracurriculars :

Biggest accomplishment this year :

Highlight of the school year :

My Birthday!

Add Photo Here!

This is how we celebrated your birthday this year :

As you grow...

A note from:

5

fifth grade

1st Day of School

Date:

The Fifth Grade Edition

What do you want to be when you grow up and why?

How tall are you?

Favorite color :

Favorite food :

Favorite toy or possession :

Favorite book :

Favorite movie/show :

Who are your teachers this year?

What do you enjoy learning about most?

What is your favorite thing to do after school?

Who are some of your friends?

Who do you spend the most time with?

What are three words you'd use to describe yourself?

What makes you happy?

What makes you feel the most loved?

What do you like to do to make others feel loved?

Are you scared or afraid of anything?

What is your favorite thing you did this summer?

If you could have one wish, what would it be?

What are you looking forward to most this year?

Picture Day!

Picture day at school went like this :

Leave your Mark!

A project or piece of art you created this year :

Your signature :

Something memorable that happened :

New friends made this year :

Things you learned :

Extracurriculars :

Biggest accomplishment this year :

Highlight of the school year :

My Birthday!

Add Photo Here!

This is how we celebrated your birthday this year :

As you grow...

A note from:

6

Sixth grade

1st Day of School

Date:

The Sixth Grade Edition

What do you want to be when you grow up and why?

How tall are you?

Favorite color :

Favorite food :

Favorite toy or possession :

Favorite book :

Favorite movie/show :

Who are your teachers this year?

What do you enjoy learning about most?

What is your favorite thing to do after school?

Who are some of your friends?

Who do you spend the most time with?

What are three words you'd use to describe yourself?

What makes you happy?

What makes you feel the most loved?

What do you like to do to make others feel loved?

Are you scared or afraid of anything?

What is your favorite thing you did this summer?

If you could have one wish, what would it be?

What are you looking forward to most this year?

Picture Day!

Picture day at school went like this : ______________________________

____

____

Leave your Mark!

A project or piece of art you created this year :

Your signature :

Something memorable that happened :

New friends made this year :

Things you learned :

Extracurriculars :

Biggest accomplishment this year :

Highlight of the school year :

My Birthday!

Add Photo Here!

This is how we celebrated your birthday this year :

As you grow...

A note from:

seventh grade

1st Day of School

The Seventh Grade Edition

Date:

What do you want to be when you grow up and why?

How tall are you?

Favorite color :

Favorite food :

Favorite toy or possession :

Favorite book :

Favorite movie/show :

Who are your teachers this year?

What do you enjoy learning about most?

What is your favorite thing to do after school?

Who are some of your friends?

Who do you spend the most time with?

What are three words you'd use to describe yourself?

What makes you happy?

What makes you feel the most loved?

What do you like to do to make others feel loved?

Are you scared or afraid of anything?

What is your favorite thing you did this summer?

If you could have one wish, what would it be?

What are you looking forward to most this year?

Add Photo Here!

Picture Day!

Picture day at school went like this :

Leave your Mark!

A project or piece of art you created this year :

Your signature :

Something memorable that happened :

New friends made this year :

Things you learned :

Extracurriculars :

Biggest accomplishment this year :

Highlight of the school year :

My Birthday!

Add Photo Here!

This is how we celebrated your birthday this year :

As you grow...

A note from:

eighth grade

Date:

1st Day of School

The Eighth Grade Edition

What do you want to be when you grow up and why?

How tall are you?

Favorite color :

Favorite food :

Favorite toy or possession :

Favorite book :

Favorite movie/show :

Who are your teachers this year?

What do you enjoy learning about most?

What is your favorite thing to do after school?

Who are some of your friends?

Who do you spend the most time with?

What are three words you'd use to describe yourself?

What makes you happy?

What makes you feel the most loved?

What do you like to do to make others feel loved?

Are you scared or afraid of anything?

What is your favorite thing you did this summer?

If you could have one wish, what would it be?

What are you looking forward to most this year?

Picture Day!

Picture day at school went like this :

Leave your Mark!

A project or piece of art you created this year :

Your signature :

Something memorable that happened :

New friends made this year :

Things you learned :

Extracurriculars :

Biggest accomplishment this year :

Highlight of the school year :

My Birthday!

Add Photo Here!

This is how we celebrated your birthday this year :

As you grow...

A note from:

Freshman year

1st Day of School

The Freshman Year Edition

Date:

What do you want to be when you grow up and why?

How tall are you?

Favorite color :

Favorite food :

Favorite possession :

Favorite book :

Favorite movie/show :

Who are your teachers this year?

What do you enjoy learning about most?

What is your favorite thing to do after school?

Who are some of your friends?

Who do you spend the most time with?

What are three words you'd use to describe yourself?

What makes you happy?

What makes you feel the most loved?

What do you like to do to make others feel loved?

Are you scared or afraid of anything?

What is your favorite thing you did this summer?

If you could have one wish, what would it be?

What are you looking forward to most this year?

Picture Day!

Picture day at school went like this : ______________________________

____

____

Leave your Mark!

A project or piece of art you created this year :

Your signature :

Something memorable that happened :

New friends made this year :

Things you learned :

Extracurriculars :

Biggest accomplishment this year :

Highlight of the school year :

My Birthday!

Add Photo Here!

This is how we celebrated your birthday this year :

As you grow...

A note from:

10

Sophomore year

Date:

1st Day of School

The Sophomore Year Edition

What do you want to be when you grow up and why?

How tall are you?

Favorite color :

Favorite food :

Favorite possession :

Favorite book :

Favorite movie/show :

Who are your teachers this year?

What do you enjoy learning about most?

What is your favorite thing to do after school?

Who are some of your friends?

Who do you spend the most time with?

What are three words you'd use to describe yourself?

What makes you happy?

What makes you feel the most loved?

What do you like to do to make others feel loved?

Are you scared or afraid of anything?

What is your favorite thing you did this summer?

If you could have one wish, what would it be?

What are you looking forward to most this year?

Add Photo Here!

Picture Day!

Picture day at school went like this :

Leave your Mark!

A project or piece of art you created this year :

Your signature :

Something memorable that happened :

New friends made this year :

Things you learned :

Extracurriculars :

Biggest accomplishment this year :

Highlight of the school year :

Thoughts on a driver's license :

My Birthday!

Add Photo Here!

This is how we celebrated your birthday this year :

As you grow...

A note from:

11

junior year

1st Day of School

Date:

The Junior Year Edition

What do you want to be when you grow up and why?

How tall are you?

Favorite color :

Favorite food :

Favorite possession :

Favorite book :

Favorite movie/show :

Who are your teachers this year?

What do you enjoy learning about most?

What is your favorite thing to do after school?

Who are some of your friends?

Who do you spend the most time with?

What are three words you'd use to describe yourself?

What makes you happy?

What makes you feel the most loved?

What do you like to do to make others feel loved?

Are you scared or afraid of anything?

What is your favorite thing you did this summer?

If you could have one wish, what would it be?

What are you looking forward to most this year?

Picture Day!

Picture day at school went like this :

Leave your Mark!

A project or piece of art you created this year :

Your signature :

Something memorable that happened :

New friends made this year :

Things you learned :

Extracurriculars :

Biggest accomplishment this year :

Highlight of the school year :

Did you have a job outside of school?

My Birthday!

Add Photo Here!

This is how we celebrated your birthday this year :

As you grow...

A note from:

12

senior year

1st Day of School

The Senior Year Edition

Date:

What do you want to be when you grow up and why?

How tall are you?

Favorite color :

Favorite food :

Favorite possession :

Favorite book :

Favorite movie/show :

Who are your teachers this year?

What do you enjoy learning about most?

What is your favorite thing to do after school?

Who are some of your friends?

Who do you spend the most time with?

What are three words you'd use to describe yourself?

What makes you happy?

What makes you feel the most loved?

What do you like to do to make others feel loved?

Are you scared or afraid of anything?

What is your favorite thing you did this summer?

If you could have one wish, what would it be?

What are you looking forward to most this year?

Picture Day!

Picture day at school went like this : ______________________________

____

____

Leave your Mark!

A project or piece of art you created this year :

Your signature :

Something memorable that happened :

New friends made this year :

Things you learned :

Extracurriculars :

Biggest accomplishment this year :

Highlight of the school year :

Plans after graduation :

My Birthday!

Add Photo Here!

This is how we celebrated your birthday this year :

As you grow...

A note from:

Add Photo Here!

Leaving the Nest

OTHER GIFTABLE BOOKS BY KORIE HEROLD

***OUR BUCKET LIST ADVENTURES* :** Whether you dream of a big trip abroad or doing smaller activities together in your own town, use this journal to keep track of all the things you and your partner hope to do one day.

***OUR CHRISTMAS STORY : A MODERN MEMORY BOOK FOR CHRISTMAS* -** Write down meaningful holiday traditions, record special gifts given or received, save photos with Santa or annual family Christmas cards, preserve treasured family holiday recipes, and so much more! This book makes for a thoughtful gift for a bridal shower, wedding gift, or for a family who loves to celebrate Christmas.

***AROUND OUR TABLE : A MODERN HEIRLOOM RECIPE BOOK TO ORGANIZE AND PRESERVE YOUR FAMILY'S MOST CHERISHED MEALS* -** Preserve all of your favorite recipes, and the memories associated with them, in this heirloom-quality blank recipe book that includes 7 sections to organize your recipes, along with recipe cards, plastic sleeves to preserve new and old recipes, and a pocket folder in the back for additional storage.

***GROWING YOU : A KEEPSAKE PREGNANCY JOURNAL AND MEMORY BOOK FOR MOM & BABY* -** *Growing You* is an heirloom-quality book to celebrate and chronicle your pregnancy journey, reflecting on the growth, anticipation, and memories that you want to hold onto as a mother. This journal is the perfect gift for someone early on in their pregnancy.

***AS YOU GROW : A MODERN MEMORY BOOK FOR BABY* -** A modern take on a baby memory book and journal, *As You Grow* stands out from the crowd of baby books with its elegant, chic, and timeless design. The gender-neutral artwork with guided sections provide space for every family to record moments from pregnancy to age five.

***GRATEFUL FOR YOU : A GRATITUDE JOURNAL FOR PARENTS TO PRESERVE MEMORIES AND SPECIAL MOMENTS* -** *Grateful For You* is a short form, easy memory book to fill out for your child over the years. The journal is undated so there's no pressure on the frequency you write inside, and each entry has space for only a sentence or two. This book is written through the lens of gratitude.

***AS WE GROW : A MODERN MEMORY BOOK FOR MARRIED COUPLES* -** *As We Grow* is a place to celebrate and remember the details of your marriage. Record the story of how you live and love and preserve it in writing—a treasure you can pass to your children and grandchildren. It's the perfect gift for the newly engaged couple, the newly married couple, or those who have been married for years!

***MOM'S/DAD'S STORY : A MEMORY AND KEEPSAKE JOURNAL FOR MY FAMILY* -** These two guided journals provide parents with thoughtful writing prompts to help them record their most precious moments and pass them down to their families.

***GRANDMA'S/GRANDPA'S STORY : A MEMORY AND KEEPSAKE JOURNAL FOR MY FAMILY* -** These two guided journals provide grandparents with thoughtful writing prompts to help them record their most precious moments and pass them down to their grandchildren and families. Beautifully designed keepsake journals, these books are the perfect gift for Mother's/Father's Day, birthdays, or any special occasion.

***MORE THAN GRATITUDE* -** Spend 100 days cultivating deep roots of gratitude through guided journaling, prayer, and scripture. *More Than Gratitude* is ready to meet you where you are, and help you grow in your daily walk with the Lord, through six simple daily prompts. Grab your sisters, neighbors, friends, and family and do this journey together!

SPECIAL THANKS

My husband—*I'm looking at you, Joel. Your constant support and encouragement to keep on creating is what keeps me going. You fuel my fire and I'm so grateful for you. Thank you for creating a safe space for me to chase my dreams, one after the next.*

Xander and Jonah—*Boys, this book is for you. I look forward to watching each of you grow into sweet young men, and I already cherish the fleeting moments I get with you while you're young little sponges living in our home. I pray we pass down love, kindness, and determination to chase wild dreams to each of you.*

Paige Tate & Co.—*Thank you for consistently encouraging me to create books I want to see more of in the world. You know this wouldn't be possible without you. I am so grateful you answered my email all those years ago and said "yes" to this journey with me. Thank you for allowing my voice and vision to shine through, and more importantly, thank you for your friendship along the way. Y'all are the best kind of people.*

Growing Up

A MODERN MEMORY BOOK FOR THE SCHOOL YEARS

Inside This Pocket